FAVORITE HORSE BREEDS

APPALOOSA HORSES

by Cari Meister

AMICUS | AMICUS INK

Amicus High Interest and Amicus Ink are published by Amicus
P.O. Box 1329, Mankato, MN 56002
www.amicuspublishing.us

Library of Congress Cataloging-in-Publication Data
Names: Meister, Cari, author.
Title: Appaloosa horses / by Cari Meister.
Description: Mankato, Minnesota : Amicus/Amicus Ink, [2019] | Series:
  Favorite horse breeds | Audience: Grade K to grade 3. | Includes index.
Identifiers: LCCN 2017028763 (print) | LCCN 2017031606 (ebook) | ISBN
  9781681515052 (pdf) | ISBN 9781681514239 (library bound) | ISBN
  9781681523439 (paperback) | ISBN 9781681515052 (ebook)
Subjects: LCSH: Appaloosa horse--Juvenile literature.
Classification: LCC SF293.A7 (ebook) | LCC SF293.A7 M45 2019 (print) |
  DDC 636.1/3--dc23
LC record available at https://lccn.loc.gov/2017028763

Photo Credits: jeanma85/iStock cover; GlobalP/iStock 2; Gerard Lacz/
mauritius images GmbH/Alamy 5; Marilyn Angel Wynn/Nativestock/
Getty 6; Picsoftheday/Shutterstock 8–9; Mark J. Barrett/Alamy 10–11, 12–
13; Lenkadan/Shutterstock 14–15; pmcdonald/iStock 16; AfricanWildcat/
Shutterstock 18–19; Tierfotoagentur/M. Hannawacker/Alamy 21; Eric
Isselee/Shutterstock 22

Editor: Wendy Dieker
Designer: Veronica Scott
Photo Researcher: Holly Young

Printed in China

HC 10 9 8 7 6 5 4 3 2 1
PB 10 9 8 7 6 5 4 3 2 1

TABLE OF CONTENTS

STRONG AND SPOTTED

A spotted horse trots up a hill. He runs past the woods. The horse is strong and fit. He runs and runs. He is an Appaloosa.

Did You Know?
People call these horses Appys for short.

4

NATIVE HISTORY

The Appy breed traces back to early America. In the 1700s, the **Nez Perce** people mixed Spanish horses with other horses. They wanted a fast, sturdy horse. They got it!

SPOTTED HUNTER

Native hunters loved this spotted horse. Appys were good on the hunt. They were fast. They could go and go. Their spots helped them hide.

Did You Know?
Some Appys have a leopard pattern. It is white with small dark spots all over.

MANY PATTERNS

This horse is known for its patterns. A horse may have big spots. It may have sprinkles of another color. It may have a **blanket pattern**. No two horses are alike.

MANY COLORS

Appaloosa horses have a **base color**. Appys can have one of 13 base colors. They range from white to gray to black. Some are shades of brown.

Did You Know?
Some Appys are all one color. This is rare. Almost all have spots or markings.

12

CHANGING COLORS

Baby Appys are soft and fuzzy. The **foal**'s coat will shed as it grows. The new coat may come in darker. The spots may get bigger. There is no way to know until the foal grows up.

DOTTED SKIN

Look at the Appy's **muzzle**. Look under the tail. The skin has little dots. This is called **mottled** skin. Few breeds have skin like this. It is an Appy trait.

STRIPED HOOVES

Appaloosas can have striped hooves. The hoof is the horny part of the foot. Do you see the stripes? The lines can be light or dark. They can be thick or thin.

STAR OF THE SHOW

An Appy is smart. She learns fast. She can be trained to do many things. You might see an Appy at a horse show. Appys can even be trained to be in movies.

HOW DO YOU KNOW IT'S AN APPALOOSA HORSE?

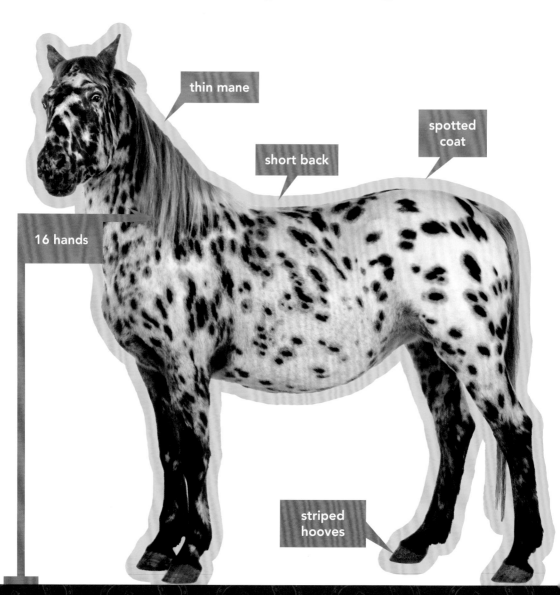

thin mane

spotted coat

short back

16 hands

striped hooves

WORDS TO KNOW

base color – the main coat color of a horse; spots and markings appear to be on top of the base color.

blanket pattern – a solid or spotted white area that looks like a blanket covering the horse's coat.

foal – a baby horse.

mottled – covered with small spots or markings.

muzzle – the nose and mouth of a horse.

Nez Perce – Native Americans who live in the Pacific Northwest area of the United States.

LEARN MORE

Books

Dell, Pamela. *Appaloosas*. North Mankato, Minn.: Child's World, 2014.

Kolpin, Molly. *Favorite Horses: Breeds Girls Love*. North Mankato, Minn.: Capstone, 2015.

Websites

Appaloosa Youth Association
http://www.appaloosayouth.com/

Horse Channel | Field Guide to Appaloosa Coat Patterns
http://www.horsechannel.com/horse-breeds/a-field-guide-to-appaloosa-coat-patterns.aspx

INDEX